Answers About
DINOSAURS and
PREHISTORIC MAMMALS

Written by FREDERICK SMITHLINE

Illustrated by JOHN HULL
KENYON SHANNON
R. F. PETERSON

Design and editorial production by
DONALD D. WOLF and MARGOT L. WOLF

GROSSET & DUNLAP · Publishers · NEW YORK

CONTENTS

WHAT IS PREHISTORIC LIFE?

History means "a record of past events." Since *pre* means "before," you can see that *prehistoric* means "before a record of past events." More accurately, *prehistoric* means "before a *written* record of past events," because events that took place in past ages of the earth have left clear and abundant records, and one of these records is in the form of fossils.

A fossil is preserved evidence of prehistoric plant or animal life. Hard parts of animals, such as teeth, bones, and shells have been buried by layers of sediment that later turned to rock. The encasing rock preserved these animal parts from decay. Millions of years afterward, when the rock weathered away, the teeth, bones, and shells could be found in nearly the same condition as when their owners died. Whole skeletons of animals have been found preserved in this way.

Fossil shown at left is a plant impression encased in rock.

HOW DID AMBER CREATE FOSSILS?

INSECT FOSSIL IN AMBER

Sometimes whole plants or animals have become fossils by being trapped in some substance that preserved them from decay. Amber is one such substance. Amber looks like clear, dark-yellow plastic. Amber is itself a fossil of the sticky yellow pitch that oozed from the bark of pine trees.

Fossils of insects, leaves, and twigs have been found encased in amber. These living things became caught in the sticky pitch on the trunks and limbs of trees, and after a time, were covered completely by the oozing pitch. Long contact with the air hardened the pitch. The trees died, fell, and decayed. The hardened pitch was buried in the earth, and eventually became amber.

Prehistoric North American tar pits, such as the La Brea Tar Pits of California, were filled with a sticky mixture of soil and petroleum that were often death-traps.

WHAT DID THE TAR PITS AND "DEEP FREEZES" REVEAL?

Tar and asphalt are substances that can preserve animal remains from decay. Thousands of skeletons of animals have been found in tar and asphalt pits which may at one time have been covered by water. Animals drinking this water became stuck in the tar and were unable to pull themselves free. These trapped animals sank beneath the surface of the tar. The tar hardened to asphalt and preserved the animals buried in it. The Rancho La Brea Tar Pits, near Los Angeles, California, are famous for the thousands of beautifully preserved skeletons that have been dug out of them. Horses, mammoths, wolves, saber-toothed cats, and vultures are among the animals that were trapped in these tar pits.

Ice is another substance that has preserved animal remains. In Alaska and Siberia, whole carcasses of mammoths and rhinoceroses have been found in frozen mud. Bones, skin, hair, toenails, internal organs, and even food in the stomachs of these fossil animals were preserved.

9

**ONE-CELLED
LIVING
MATTER**

WHERE DID LIFE ON EARTH BEGIN?

In the beginning there had been life only in the seas. That is where life first started. The first living things of which we have records were algae, sponges, and possibly some kind of worm. However, in the warm seas of this very early time there were probably many other kinds of living things. The rocks formed then are found among the deepest sedimentary rocks. They have been broken and covered by igneous rocks many times. So, it is easy to see that, even if most of the living things of this time were not too soft-bodied to form fossils, it still would be difficult to find fossils of them. Because of the lack of fossils, this period of the earth's history has been named the *Cryptozoic Eon* (krip-to-zo-ik EE-on). *Cryptozoic* means "hidden animal life," and an *eon* is a long period of time of no exact length.

WHAT WERE TRILOBITES?

In the warm seas that covered much of the earth, there was a great profusion of living things. Chief among them were *trilobites* (TRY-lo-bites), animals that got their names because their bodies were formed in three lobes; that is, they were trilobed. They had feelers protruding from beneath the fore part of their bodies, and eyes made up of a great number of lenses—in some trilobites, as many as 30,000 lenses. They had more

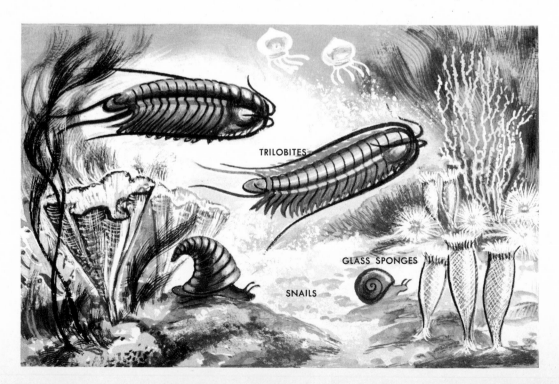

TRILOBITES

GLASS SPONGES

SNAILS

than twenty legs on each side of their bodies, and were covered with a horny material such as that which covers crabs today. They breathed through gills, as fishes do. The smallest trilobites were less than half an inch long, the longest reached a length of twenty-eight inches, but the average was about one-and-a-half inches. They were carnivorous, which means that they ate other animals.

Besides trilobites, there were many kinds of sponges and corals in the seas. There were clamlike shellfish that were preyed upon by star-fish. Small centipede-like creatures crawled on the sea bottom, and jelly-fish floated in the water above. A most unusual animal was the *crinoid* that looked just like a graceful plant. It stood on a long stalk that rested on the sea bottom. Of course, the stalk had no roots.

WHEN DID THE FIRST FISH APPEAR?

The 40-million-year period that began 360 million years ago is the *Silurian* (sih-LOO-ree-in) *Period.* All animal life still lived in the seas. The nautilids decreased greatly in number, and those surviving had coiled and frilled shells. Crinoids, many beautifully colored, still waved about on stalks in response to currents at the bottom of the sea. King crabs appeared, and they have changed but little in all the hundreds of millions of years from the Silurian Period to the present. The first fish appeared, too. There were many kinds, none more than three or four inches long. Some trilobites still crawled on the sea bottom. But the form of life that dominated this period was the sea scorpion. These sea-living animals looked very much like the scorpions that live on land today. There were many kinds of sea scorpions, varying in length from two-inch pygmies to nine-foot giants.

About 350 million years ago the first living things appeared on land. They were mosses, much like those we see today.

At the end of the Silurian Period, about 320 million years ago, mosses developed into new kinds of plants. These were merely branching stems, without leaves or roots, not more than eight inches tall. They were soon followed by ferns.

WHAT CHANGES OCCURRED ON LAND DURING THE DEVONIAN PERIOD?

The period that began 320 million years ago and lasted 55 million years is the *Devonian* (dee-vo-nian) *Period*. This period brought about a dramatic change on the land areas of the world. The mosses and ferns developed into plants of many different kinds and covered the naked rocks of the land with a carpet of green. As the new plants died by the millions, their decaying remains mixed with grains of sediment left by the retreating seas, and the first real soil was formed.

DEVONIAN SEA

LOWER DEVONIAN LANDSCAPE

In this soil, ever more abundant plants grew. The soil was able to hold moisture as well as minerals needed by plants. As plants helped to form soil in which to grow, they were able gradually to grow farther and farther away from shore. Ferns developed into treelike plants, and toward the end of the Devonian Period, some of these had simple leaves. All the many different kinds of plants reproduced by means of spores—just as today's ferns do. The spores were carried by wind and water, and plants sprang up in new locations. However, in order that plants may grow from spores, much water is needed, so it was only in rainy seasons that spores could develop into plants in inland areas. In Devonian time, the climate was usually mild and wet all over the world.

WHAT WAS AN EARLY LARGE FISH?

In the seas, many kinds of large fish appeared and grew in great numbers during the Devonian Period. Many of these fish fed on trilobites, and nearly wiped out these early animals. There were scaly fish, smooth-skinned fish, and armored fish. Among these fish were the first sharks. Indeed, fish dominated the seas, so the Devonian Period is also called the Age of Fishes.

One of the largest fish was *Dinichthys* (din-IK-thees), a name that means "terrible fish." *Dinichthys* grew to be twenty feet long, and one-third of this length was an armored head. Its powerful jaws had four large, bony teeth set in sharp, bony ridges, and could snap shut like a big pair of shears. Surely, *Dinichthys* was feared by other sea dwellers of Devonian time.

Some scientists contend that lungfishes were the first animals to adapt from life in the sea to life on land.

WHAT WAS THE FIRST LAND ANIMAL?

During the Devonian Period, the first land animals appeared. The first animal to live on land came out of the sea. We do not know just what this animal was. Some scientists think it was a sea scorpion; others think it was a lungfish, because a lungfish has gills that enable it to live under water as fish do, and lungs that enable it to breathe air, as land animals do. Still other scientists believe that the first land animal was one of the centipede-like creatures that lived in the sea.

Whichever may have been first, descendants of all three kinds of animals were living on land by the end of the Devonian Period. The lungfish developed strong fins with which it could push itself about on mud-flats during dry seasons. In later lungfish generations these strong fins developed into legs of the lungfish's descendant, the first *amphibian* (am-FIB-ee-un). From sea scorpions and sea centipedes came land-living scorpions and centipedes, and from these came spiders, and finally, true insects.

From nearly bare land to green forests, from fins and gills in the sea to legs and lungs on land—these were the changes wrought by the slow passage of the 55 million years of the Devonian Period. There were greater changes during this period than in any other time of equal length in the history of the earth.

WHAT WERE THE FIRST AMPHIBIANS?

After the Devonian Period, about 320 million years ago, the Coal Age started. This was the time when the coal deposits of North America were formed, when the seas teemed with sharks and the land was covered with thick forests, inhabited by amphibians, descendants of the lungfish.

An early amphibian creature who spent most of his days in shallow water was one who in time would be given the name *Diplocaulus* (dip-luh-KAWL-us). Both his body and skull were broad and flat. It is estimated that he was about two feet long. When he swam about in water along the muddy shoreline, his tail proved exceptionally useful, but he was hampered considerably on land by small weak legs that did not take him very far without undue exertion. It is little wonder that he was never able to develop his lung-breathing, the one characteristic that distinguishes land animals from sea creatures.

Diplocaulus—his name means "double shaft" or "stalk," because that best describes the formation of his vertebrae—had a large triangular-shaped head, marked by pointed winglike protuberances at each side.

Because his movements were limited on land, and because other amphibians eventually developed stronger legs and backbones for adventuresome mobility outside the water environment, *Diplocaulus* could not long survive, and he and his kind gradually became extinct.

About 200 million years ago, Diplocaulus, a two-foot prehistoric salamander, lived in what is today the northern part of Texas. At left, an artist's conception; at right, a skeleton found in Texas.

WHAT WAS ONE OF THE LARGEST AMPHIBIANS?

Above, a dragonfly, trapped during the Coal Age and preserved as a fossil.

In the forests and swamps of the Coal Age, amphibians such as Eryops ran or swam about, and giant insects such as Meganeuron flew through the humid air.

One of the largest of the amphibians, and one who must have presented a formidable appearance in his day, was *Eryops* (ER-ee-ops), a meat-eating creature with an enormous mouth and long sharp teeth. By present-day comparisons, he was very much like a crocodile, reaching a length of perhaps nine feet. He had a long, heavy tail which was more hindrance than help, for it was merely something to "drag along" as he crawled about clumsily on short but powerful legs. It did not contribute anything particularly useful toward his survival.

Paleontologists and other scientists in allied fields speculated for a long time as to what this particular amphibian's skin was like. Was it smooth? Or was it rough and pebbly in texture? The answer came when some fossil remains of *Eryops* were found in the state of Texas. Careful examination of the rock in which a mummified specimen was encased disclosed telltale impressions of the creature's skin. The texture might best be described as leathery. The scientific investigation also revealed small, flat, bony scales within the leathery skin.

(Harvard University, Cambridge, Massachusetts, houses a collection of fossil remains in which this unusual specimen is included. The university each year plays host to thousands of visitors who come to view the interesting exhibit.)

Eryops' eggs were always laid in water; and, like fish eggs, they had a soft covering, instead of the shell-like casing that is found in birds' eggs. When the eggs hatched, the young of the species spent their first days in the surrounding water and then, eventually, crawled out onto the shore.

Once on land, however, the maturing *Eryops* could never stray very far from the water, where new eggs would again have to be laid, and the reproductive cycle would begin all over. This was something of a disadvantage. Geological changes took place, and in the natural course of events most of the earth's inland waters and swamps dried out. The consequences were fatal to *Eryops* and many other amphibians.

WHAT WAS THE ANCESTOR OF THE REPTILES?

There was one hardy amphibian who ultimately was able to lay eggs on dry land. It was very probably small in size, but this and other factors were helpful to survival. This amphibian was the forerunner of all the great reptiles that came later.

Texas was the site of an important discovery. It was near a town called Seymour in the northern part of the state. The fossil remains of a lizard-like creature about two and a half feet long were unearthed, and proved to be an evolutionary "missing link" between amphibians and reptiles. One is hard put to say whether it was an amphibian about to become a reptile or whether it was a reptile that had simply ceased being amphibious. At any rate, scientists gave it the name *Seymouria* (see-MOOR-ee-uh), relating it to the name of the neighboring town in Texas. They agreed on

The discovery of Seymouria created much excitement among scientists, since it was considered a "missing link" between amphibians and reptiles.

this, even though they could not agree on what group of animal life—amphibians or reptiles—it properly belonged.

Seymouria was similar to amphibian ancestors in that it had a broad, flat head, widespread legs and a tadpole tail, but a distinctively reptilian backbone.

The first completely land-living animals were called reptiles, which means "those who crawl." There were many different reptile families. There were the turtles, the snakes and the lizards. And there was also the reptile family which included the dinosaurs.

WHAT DOES "DINOSAUR" MEAN?

About a hundred years ago, scientists in England discovered some very large and very old skeleton remains of giant animals. After much consideration, they named the animals dinosaurs, derived from two Greek words that mean "terrible lizards."

WERE DINOSAURS ON THE NORTH AMERICAN CONTINENT?

One day, nearly a hundred years ago, some workmen were digging a foundation for a building in a little town in New Jersey. As they dug deep into the dirt and rock, they came upon what seemed to be huge bones and teeth. The bones and teeth were so hard that they looked as if they had turned into stone.

"Very strange," the workers said as they examined these giant bones. "Too big for a cow or a horse. They're even too big for an elephant!"

The workmen tossed the bones aside and got on with their job of digging. But some of the men brought a few of the strange bones home as souvenirs. People in the neighborhood heard about them, and they came by where the men were digging to get a souvenir, too. Those enormous teeth made interesting paperweights, and the big stony bones were heavy enough to use as doorstops.

But finally a famous scientist, Dr. Joseph Leidy, in nearby Philadelphia, heard about these giant bones. He hurried down to get the rest of them, because he had the very exciting thought that the bones dug up by the New Jersey workmen were dinosaur bones. After many months, Dr. Leidy put the bones together. But he found that many parts were missing.

Back to New Jersey he went, canvassing the houses to see if anyone had interesting paperweights, doorstops or other souvenirs from the digging. People were helpful about giving them up or selling them when they learned why the scientist needed the old bones.

At last Dr. Leidy fitted together a giant skeleton. This proved to be the skeleton of a duck-billed dinosaur, the *Trachodon*, the very first dinosaur skeleton found in the United States. It stands today in the Philadelphia Academy of Natural Sciences.

Since that time, there have been hundreds of dinosaur skeletons dug up in various parts of the United States. And in many of our cities there are museums where you can see these "skeleton zoos" of animals that lived millions of years ago. (Dinosaurs lived on this earth 200 million years ago, to be exact.)

HOW DID DINOSAURS GET THEIR NAMES?

One of the BIG things about dinosaurs is their names. Now there's a reason—a good reason—for these long tongue-twisters. Scientists name all plants and animals by putting together Latin and Greek words that tell something about the plant or animal. That becomes the scientific name for it in all countries, whatever their language. So scientists all over the world understand one another when it comes to scientific names.

When you learn the names of these dinosaurs, you can be sure that

Brontosaurus
(Jurassic Period)

Iguanodon
(Cretaceous Period)

Trachodon
(Cretaceous Period)

boys and girls in France or Russia or Germany or South America are calling them by the very same names. Take the dinosaur *Brontosaurus* (bron-tuh-SOR-us), for example. That means "thunder lizard." *Iguanodon* (ih-GWAN-uh-don) means "iguana lizard" and "tooth." And now that you understand it, you will find it as easy to rattle off as "hippopotamus" (which means "river horse," by the way).

Each time you see a dinosaur name, remember that it usually means something simple that describes the animal.

WHAT WERE SOME OF THE EARLIEST REPTILES?

One of the earliest reptiles to live on our planet was *Edaphosaurus* (ee-daf-uh-SOR-us), whose scientific name means "foundation," or "base lizard." His name was probably derived from the fact that he looked like a long-tailed lizard. More accurately, because of an odd sail on his back, he looked like a sailing ship. His fossil remains were found amid the red sandstone of Texas.

Dinosaurs did not appear on earth suddenly. They developed slowly from one of the reptile families during the great Age of Reptiles.

EDAPHOSAURUS

This reptile was herbivorous—that is to say, he subsisted on plants that grew along the shores of streams and lakes. He had small teeth around the edges of his jaws, but for extracting juice from plants that grew in abundance he had crushing teeth that were quite useful.

Another early reptile—whose name means "double-measure tooth"—was *Dimetrodon* (dye-MET-ruh-don). His jaws were filled with two different sizes of teeth, sharp dagger points that could puncture and tear away flesh like a knife. He had a large skull and jaws and his terrifying appearance with not without some justification, for he was indeed a meat-eater. Like *Edaphosaurus*, he also had a large, curved "sail" on his back. It is not known for certain just what purpose this odd attachment served for either reptile. Some scientists theorize that the sail was an "air-conditioner" that regulated body temperature in some manner. On the other hand, it may have been utterly useless—a decorative embellishment without function.

Ironically, though *Dimetrodon* and his reptilian cousin *Edaphosaurus* had this odd back-sail in common, and lived in much the same places, they played the competitive roles of hunter and hunted. *Edaphosaurus* was usually the victim of *Dimetrodon's* carnivorous attacks.

DIMETRODONS

WERE PEOPLE LIVING DURING THE TIME OF THE DINOSAURS?

Dinosaurs lived and died long, long before the first man appeared on earth, which happened during the Pleistocene Epoch less than a million years ago. And it's amazing to think that only human beings living in the past hundred years or so have even known or seen what a dinosaur looked like! Though the dinosaurs themselves are very, very old, the science that tells us about them is quite new. And while we have been learning new things about outer space and planets and preparing for the new space age to come, we have also been discovering new things about this old earth and what it was like millions of years ago.

Saltoposuchus was the "great-grandfather" of the giant dinosaurs, although measuring less than four feet itself.

WERE ALL DINOSAURS BIG?

At first, dinosaurs were small creatures not more than two or three feet long. They were cold-blooded like the other reptiles, but instead of crawling along the ground on four legs, the early dinosaurs scampered along on their hind legs. Their small front legs had clawlike hands, and they balanced themselves by means of a long, skinny, lizard-like tail.

Though these early dinosaurs were small, they were fierce. They were meat-eaters who fed on other small reptiles. Because of their speed, and because they used their front legs for grasping and tearing their prey, they had a big advantage. Their small four-legged neighbors didn't stand a chance against them.

22

Camptosaurus means "bent" or "flexible lizard." The dinosaur was given that name because it could walk on its large hind legs, or bend down and walk on all fours. Camptosaurus was a plant-eater, and not very large.

WERE ALL DINOSAURS MEAT-EATERS?

Some of the dinosaurs grew larger and continued to scurry through the leafy green plants hunting down other animals. These meat-eaters, no matter how large they grew, always walked on their powerful hind legs. Their forelegs remained like tiny arms held close to their chest.

But some of the early dinosaurs developed differently. Over many, many years, they lived on a rich diet of plants. The world was carpeted with juicy green leaves, and a plant-eating animal could spend its whole life just in eating. By and by, some of these plant-eaters grew to enormous size.

Finally, the plant-eating dinosaurs had to drop down to a four-legged position. In the first place, it was easier to reach the plants that way. In the second place, they were getting too heavy to support their weight on two legs. As a matter of fact, it wasn't always easy to carry all those pounds around on four legs! So some of the largest plant-eaters spent a good bit of time in water. This helped them hold up their weight, because their great bodies could float partly in the water.

Also, when the gentle plant-eaters were in the water, they were safe from their fierce two-legged, meat-eating cousins. The two-legged dinosaurs didn't dare to do more than get their big hind feet wet, even when they saw a delicious dinosaur dinner just a little way out in the lake. And that was a lucky thing for the plant-eaters. Since they were slow and clumsy, and did not have sharp teeth or claws, the lakes and lagoons were all that saved them from the terrible hunters on land.

Brachiosaurus

WHICH DINOSAUR WAS THE BIGGEST?

Brachiosaurus (brak-ee-uh-SOR-us), a giant among giants, got his name from two Greek words meaning "arm lizard." The bones of his fore-arm were unusually large.

Brachiosaurus was the biggest and heaviest of all the dinosaurs. He was so tall that his little head could easily have looked over a three-story building. Most dinosaurs had longer hind legs than forelegs, but this one was built differently. His long neck went straight up, too.

Brachiosaurus was so heavy—he weighed 100,000 pounds—that he could barely drag himself around on land, so he couldn't fight or run away from his enemies. Therefore, he spent nearly all of his time in the water. He was able to go out into very deep water and still keep his head above the surface. That was where the long neck and long front legs were a help.

There was something else unusual about this biggest dinosaur. At the very top of his head he had a dome with nostrils in it. *Brachiosaurus* could stay hidden under water with just this little breathing dome showing.

There were plenty of water plants for him to feed on. And this great clumsy creature spent most of his time standing in water, chewing on plants. He couldn't move around much on land. He couldn't swim in the water. It must have been a dull way to live—even for a dinosaur.

WHY DID SOME DINOSAURS HAVE ARMOR?

Ankylosaurus (an-kil-uh-SOR-us), which means "curved lizard," got his name because of the way his ribs curved heavily over his back. He was an example of another way the plant-eaters could defend themselves against the meat-eaters. *Ankylosaurus* wore armor. He was the walking tank of his time, reaching a length of ten feet.

Ankylosaurus did not have to live near the water for safety, as his other relatives did. As a matter of fact, he would have sunk like a stone if he had ever tried hiding in the water! This armored dinosaur was quite safe from the meat-eaters. Even their sharp teeth and claws could not get at *his* meat, which was locked in bone.

The back of *Ankylosaurus* was covered with bony plates that protected him. They curved over him like a turtle's shell. Then he had long spikes that stuck out from the sides of his body and protected his short legs. Even his head had a bony covering, which served as a kind of helmet.

Most useful of all was the marvelous tail of this armored dinosaur. It was covered with rings of bone. At the end of the tough, hard tail was a great lump of bone. Any meat-eater who challenged this dinosaur would get a strong whack from that heavy tail. It was enough to send the hunter away to look for an easier meal.

These dinosaurs lived on the higher dry land, away from swamps and marshes. Every kind of dinosaur had his own favorite place to live. There would have been no balance of life if they all wanted to live in water, or if they all wanted to live on dry land. So each found his own best place, and after millions of years their bodies changed to fit their kind of life.

In that way there was enough room and enough food for everyone. And because of their different lives they developed into many different kinds of creatures.

ANKYLOSAURUS

HOW DID STYRACOSAURUS USE ITS SPIKES?

Styracosaurus (sty-rak-uh-SOR-us), which means "spiked lizard," measured almost 25 feet in length. Six spiked horns protruded from the top of his armor-plated head, and a large, pointed horn grew out of his forehead. Inasmuch as *Styracosaurus* was a plant-eater who fought only when attacked, the horns were used more often for defense than for

Styracosaurus, a plant-eater, lived about 90 million years ago.

offense. In any event, these horns, combined with an extremely tough skin, served as excellent protection against the many ferocious meat-eaters of the time. Fossil remains of *Styracosaurus* were found on the North American continent, mainly in the province of Alberta in Canada and the state of Montana in the United States.

WHICH DINOSAUR WAS THE LONGEST?

Diplodocus (dih-PLOD-uh-kuss) got his name from two Greek words meaning "double beam." Take a look at him and you'll know why. He had a body with two long beams sticking out—one in front and one in back. And it wasn't very easy to tell which beam had the brain.

Like the other big plant-eating dinosaurs who waded in the swamps and lakes, *Diplodocus* had a very small head. Scientists are puzzled about how that tiny mouth and narrow neck could let him get enough food down to feed his big body. *Diplodocus* was the longest of the dinosaurs, but he was lighter and thinner than his big relatives. He was 87½ feet long. That's about as long as seven automobiles standing bumper to bumper! It took a lot of food to fill up an animal that size.

Diplodocus spent most of his time in the water, too. His nostrils and eyes were high up on his small head. He could keep himself well hidden under water, and his long neck could stretch way up, letting him just breathe and see. He wasn't very smart, but he knew how to hide from his enemies.

All the big, slow, wading dinosaurs were probably the first to die out. They needed low swampy land and the kind of soft plants that grew there and in the water. Their teeth weren't strong enough to chew the tougher dry plants.

After many millions of years, when the shallow water began to drain away, these gentle giants were no longer able to live on the drier land. Even if they could have gotten along on a diet of different plants, they still would have needed the swamps and lakes to hide in. If they could not plunge into water, there was no other way for them to escape the large meat-eaters.

WHICH DINOSAUR WAS THE FIERCEST?

One of the most ferocious meat-eating dinosaurs was *Allosaurus* (al-uh-SOR-us), whose name comes from two Greek words meaning "other lizard." It is a rather tame name for such a fierce beast. He was a giant meat-eating dinosaur who lived on the other giant dinosaurs of his time.

There were other, smaller meat-eaters who fed on the smaller dinosaurs, but *Allosaurus,* because of his size, was the most terrible of all. He was 35 feet long from the tip of his big tail to the front of his huge jaws.

Allosaurus had strong, heavy hind legs on which he ran. His hind feet had three clawed toes, rather like a bird's. The long tail helped him balance on two legs, like a seesaw. Up in front were two tiny arms with heavy curved claws that he could hook into his food. And his head was very large. His jaws were like a crocodile's, and his teeth were big sharp blades.

Though some of the plant-eating dinosaurs were much bigger than *Allosaurus,* they could not fight him. In the first place, he was faster than the four-legged fellows. And his big jaws, sharp teeth, and wicked claws were dangerous weapons. It is no wonder that many of the plant-eaters waded out into the water to escape *Allosaurus.*

DIPLODOCUS

ALLOSAURUS

29

WHAT IS THE BALANCE OF NATURE?

In all groups of animals that live side by side in the world, there have to be some who hunt and some who are the hunted. There must be some who eat plants and some who eat flesh. This is called the balance of nature. If all animals were plant-eaters, there would soon be too many of them. They would eat the world bare, and there would not be nough food for all. By having some animals feed on other animals, their number is kept down, and there is a balance between the kinds of animals and their food. In that way there is a chance for many kinds of life, both plant and animal, to thrive on earth.

All animals develop, for the most part, according to their eating habits. This is true among groups of animals today, and it was true millions of years ago among the different dinosaur groups. The world would have been a dinosaur heaven if it weren't for the terrible creature named *Allosaurus.*

WHICH DINOSAUR WAS THE FIRST TO BE DESCRIBED SCIENTIFICALLY?

In 1822, Dr. Gideon Mantell found some fossil teeth in Sussex, England. The teeth belonged to a dinosaur that had evolved from a rather small plant-eating ancestor. Dr. Mantell, however, erroneously imagined them to be like iguana teeth, and hence named the fossil *Iguanodon,* which is a combination of words meaning "iguana lizard" and "tooth." This name came about even before the word "dinosaur" had been invented. Some time later, in a rock quarry near the place where he had discoverd the teeth, Dr. Mantell also found some bones.

After much conjecture, Dr. Mantell began to fit the bones and teeth together as best he could, and came to the conclusion that they belonged to a new kind of giant reptile, probably about four feet long, something resembling an iguana lizard.

Skeletons of *Iguanodon* were also found in a coal mine in Belgium in 1877. A herd of the beasts had apparently dropped into a deep fissure millions of years before and had been buried in the rock ever since. Other

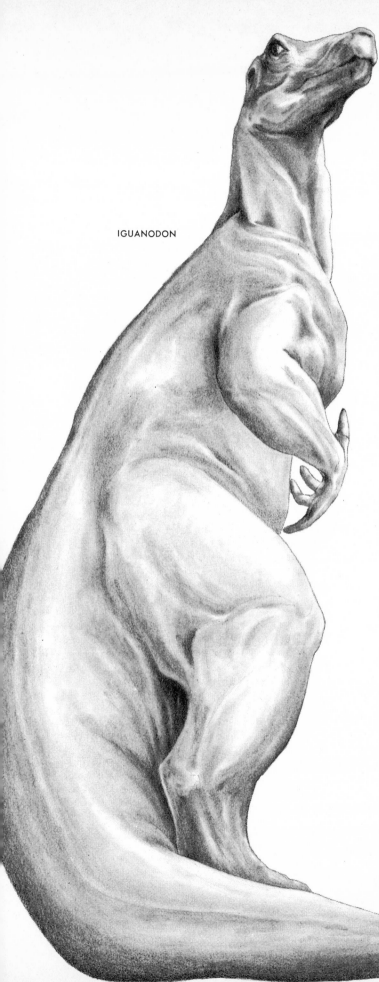

IGUANODON

skeletons were subsequently found in England, and together, these collections provided scientists with exceptional information regarding *Iguanodon's* anatomy. They could now determine that he was about thirty feet long, with a thick body and a heavy tail and neck, and that he walked on two feet. What was first thought to be a beak was really a large, spikelike "thumb."

Dr. Mantell's patience and scientific persistence was duly recognized in time and he became famous for what may be considered the first discovery of a prehistoric animal.

HOW DID "THUNDER-LIZARD" GET ITS NAME?

When the word "dinosaur" is mentioned, there comes to mind a picture of a ponderous creature having a long tail, a long neck and a small head. Such is a general description of *Brontosaurus* (bron-tuh-SOR-us), one of the best known of the gigantic plant-eating sauropods, whose legs were like pillars or tree trunks.

The scientist who named this dinosaur had a good imagination. He must have thought: "The ground probably shook and thundered every time this giant took a heavy step, so I'll call him 'thunder lizard.' "

31

Skeletons of *Brontosaurus* have been found in North America. When the scientists put the first one together, they must have been quite surprised, for there they saw an animal measuring 70 feet in length. It had a heavy tail that seemed to go on and on until it tapered off to a long thin point. Its body must have been the size of a small blimp. And four stout legs like tree trunks held it up. Then a long neck, almost as long as the tail, stretched out in front.

But strangest of all was the small head, no bigger than the neck. And the mouth that fed that whole enormous animal was quite small. In it there were about twenty-four weak, peg-shaped teeth.

Brontosaurus, the scientists decided, must have kept that little mouth busy munching plants nearly every minute. Otherwise he could never have taken in enough food to feed his huge body.

HOW BIG WAS BRONTOSAURUS?

Though *Brontosaurus* could thump around on land, nibbling at the plants that grew there, he probably was never far from the water. And he spent a good part of his time in the water, which helped support his weight of some 60,000 pounds! He was as large as seven big elephants!

When his terrible enemy, *Allosaurus,* came in sight, *Brontosaurus* would move into deeper water. He could go out rather far and still keep his head well above water. He did not even have to stop eating.

But sometimes *Brontosaurus* was up on dry land near the shore when *Allosaurus* came hunting for meat. Then there was only one thing to do. *Brontosaurus* would have to turn tail and move—as fast as his size would let him—to the safety of the lake. Maybe at those moments he was able to use his long tail like a whip and strike it against the head of the enemy that was chasing him.

HOW DO WE KNOW HOW DINOSAURS HUNTED?

At the American Museum of Natural History in New York City, you can see the record of one dinosaur chasing another. It was printed in the mud (now turned to sandstone) by the dinosaurs' feet 120 million years ago. There are the big basin-shaped footprints of *Brontosaurus*. And far-

ther back, in among the larger footprints, are the three-pointed, birdlike prints of *Allosaurus*. In a few places *Allosaurus* had even stepped into the holes made by the big feet of *Brontosaurus*.

But did he catch him? Was *Brontosaurus* eaten then and there? Or did the big peaceful fellow get into the water in the nick of time? Well, sometimes he was safe and sometimes he wasn't. In this case we will never know.

WHAT WAS THE FIRST MEMBER OF THE LAST DINOSAUR FAMILY ON EARTH?

Protoceratops (proh-toh-SER-uh tops) was the name given to a small dinosaur who, for his size, had an extremely large skull. The long name comes from three Greek words that mean "first hornface." When you look at this dinosaur's picture, you may wonder who ever decided to call him "hornface," because he had no horns on his face.

Well, *Protoceratops* was the first of a large family of horn-faced dinosaurs. But he himself never had any horns. He was also the smallest of the family, as he grew only to about five or six feet in length.

Protoceratops and his family were the last of the dinosaurs to appear on earth. They were plant-eaters and quite remarkable looking. *Protoceratops* walked on four short legs, close to the ground. He had a body like a lizard's and an unusual head. His head was large and it began with a beak like a parrot's. Then it humped up near the nose. There was a big bony collar, or frill, that curved back over his neck and shoulders.

In the great-grandchildren of *Protoceratops* the hump would become a horn. And the bony collar would grow larger on the great-grandchildren, and sometimes it would even have spikes on it. These dinosaurs developed horns and spikes as a defense against the fierce hunters who lived when they did.

HAVE DINOSAUR EGGS EVER BEEN FOUND?

The first dinosaur eggs ever to be found in modern times were the eggs of *Protoceratops*. They were found in the Gobi Desert, where an expedition found a nest of them in red sandstone. This was in the 1920's.

34

During the time that giant amphibians were still in evidence, other creatures evolved which scientists called reptiles. Above, Protoceratops and nest of eggs; below, a new Protoceratops hatching.

The eggs had a pebbly surface texture (probably leathery in life), and were about eight inches long in an elongated shape. X-ray examination subsequently disclosed that two of the cluster of eggs unearthed at the time contained an unhatched *Protoceratops*.

The scientists who studied these eggs and the area in which they were found could soon deduce that the egg-laying of the female *Protoceratops* was done in much the same way as that done by sea turtles or crocodiles today. That is, she scooped out a hollow in the sand and deposited perhaps a dozen or more of her eggs in it, whereupon she covered them up with sand, relying on the heat of the sun to hatch out the young in due time. There was no bony collar on young *Protoceratops* when he was newly hatched; it developed only as he grew older.

WHICH WAS THE LAST OF THE HORNED DINOSAURS?

Triceratops (try-SER-uh-tops) was a relative of *Protoceratops*. The name *Triceratops* means "three-horned-face." And if you count the horns, you will agree that the name is right. Old "three-horns" was the last of the horned dinosaurs, and the greatest of them all.

He was 30 feet long, and a strong fighter. Although *Triceratops* ate plants, he was not a gentle animal. Nature had given him a head full of wonderful fighting weapons. He had three sharp horns, and a bony shield that protected his head, neck and shoulders.

He was not one to let his weapons go to waste. Some of the bones

Below, skeleton of Triceratops; right, an artist's conception of the animal.

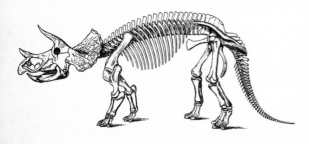

36

which were found show so many scars that we know he must have fought off the huge hunters many times.

Triceratops probably charged at his enemies fiercely, the way our present-day rhinoceros does. His neck muscles were very strong, and his big body and heavy legs had power, too.

When *Triceratops* used his swordlike horns against his enemies, the earth must have been shaken by the throes of a fight to the death.

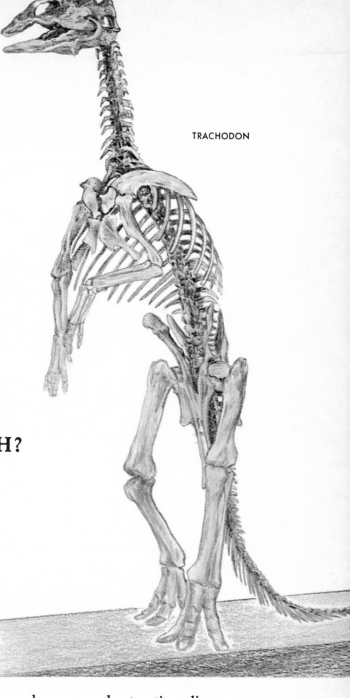

TRACHODON

WHICH OF THE DINOSAURS HAD TWO THOUSAND TEETH?

The first dinosaur whose remains were found in the United States was *Trachodon* (TRAK-uh-don), which means "rough-toothed." His teeth were described as being more like millstones, rather than daggers, as were the teeth of some of his enemies.

Trachodon had four rows of teeth that totalled two thousand in all! His teeth were for grinding, not for biting, as he was a plant-eating dinosaur. He and others like him were also known as "duck-billed dinosaurs." All duck-billed dinosaurs were descendants of *Camptosaurus,* the reptile of the late Jurassic age.

In appearance, *Trachodon* resembled his ancestor quite a bit. He had a heavy tail, which with his two hind feet served as a tripod in balancing himself. It undoubtedly also helped in his getting around in water. His feet also had become webbed, and his skull had flattened and spread into a broad bill. Apparently, these creatures spent much of their lives swimming about in water, rooting in shallow marshes and muddy bottoms with their shovel-shaped bills.

Despite his many teeth, *Trachodon* was no match for many of his flesh-eating enemies. Many *Trachodons* fell victim to the carniverous appetite of other dinosaurs, but others evidently met death in less violent ways. A number of them were mummified by nature before being buried, and impressions of their skins were eventually visible in fossile rock. From studying these impressions, scientists have been able to determine that *Trachodon's* skin was scaly and that he had webbed feet.

Some other duck-billed dinosaurs developed strange humps of bone on their skulls, and some of them grew long tubes of bone on top of their heads. These seemed to be used for breathing under water, somewhat like the snorkels that skin-divers use today.

Trachodon lived during the Mesozoic Era, 170,000,000 years ago.

WHICH DINOSAUR WAS "KING OF THE MEAT-EATERS"?

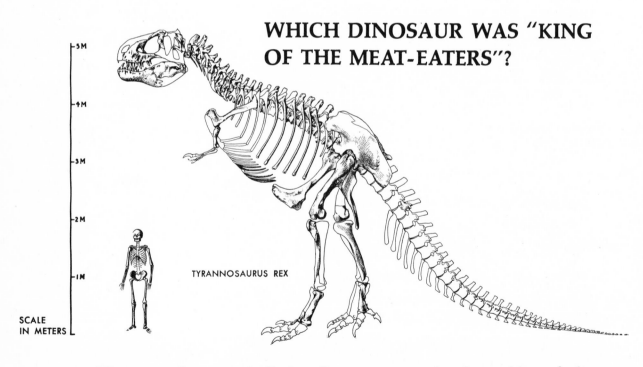

SCALE IN METERS

TYRANNOSAURUS REX

The most famous of all the dinosaurs was the fierce king of the meat-eaters, *Tyrannosaurus rex* (ty-ran-uh-SOR-us rex), which means "king of the tyrant lizards." A tyrant is a cruel ruler, so he was well-named.

Tyrannosaurus rex was the last of the great meat-eating dinosaurs, and built very much like the first little dinosaurs. You can see a close family resemblance between him and *Allosaurus,* who had lived much earlier.

But *Tyrannosaurus rex* was bigger and more terrible. His head was very large, his jaws were huge, and when they opened wide they were edged with sharp curved teeth. Some of those teeth were six inches long!

The "king of the tyrant lizards" was 45 feet long. When he stood up on his heavy hind legs he was nearly 19 feet tall. His front legs had become so small that they couldn't even reach his head. But *Tyrannosaurus rex* didn't need them. His dreadful jaws and heavy-clawed hind feet were all the weapons he needed for attacking other dinosaurs.

Tyrannosaurus rex was not afraid of any other living creature. His teeth could bite through the toughest hide and crunch the thickest bones.

WHICH DINOSAURS WERE A MATCH FOR TYRANNOSAURUS REX?

Let us try to imagine the "king of the meat-eaters" looking for food and catching sight of *Ankylosaurus,* the "curved lizard." *Tyrannosaurus rex* bounds over toward him, snapping his jaws. But the sharp teeth of the "king of the tyrant lizards" cannot bite through the heavy armor of *Ankylosaurus.*

Instead, *Ankylosaurus* swings his club of a tail. There is a sharp crack as it whacks his enemy's jaw. A tooth breaks, and *Tyrannosaurus rex* backs off, grunting in pain and anger. This creature is not good to eat!

Then *Tyrannosaurus rex* sees *Triceratops.* He takes two giant strides and he is almost upon him. But *Triceratops* is a good fighter himself. He lowers his heavy head with its shield of bone and its three sharp horns.

He charges like a rhinoceros at the much bigger *Tyrannosaurus rex.* The earth shakes as these two monsters come together. Every other sound is hushed as the two giants fight it out. *Tyrannosaurus rex* swings his great jaws open and drops down to slash at his foe's back. But *Triceratops* lunges at the soft underside of his enemy.

Both dinosaurs are wounded. *Triceratops* has a deep gash in his back. But *Tyrannosaurus rex* has been stabbed, and his breath comes in gasps.

He cannot turn and run for his life. He must obey his hunger which tells him to get meat in his jaws.

Again *Tyrannosaurus rex* snaps at the backbone of *Triceratops*. And again *Triceratops* charges with his sharp horns. The horns go deep, and the terrible *Tyrannosaurus rex* shudders and kicks as he falls dead to the ground.

But many times it was *Tyrannosaurus rex* who won and feasted on the other dinosaur. This day a lucky *Triceratops* limped away from the battlefield. He carried the scars of his victory for the rest of his life. And millions of years later, in a museum, those scars on his fossil bones tell his story to us.

TYRANNOSAURUS REX

TRICERATOPS

Triceratops, a plant-eater, was far from being a gentle animal and knew how to defend itself against carnivorous Tyrannosaurus Rex, with which it is pictured here in deadly battle.

WERE THERE SEA
AND AIR REPTILES?

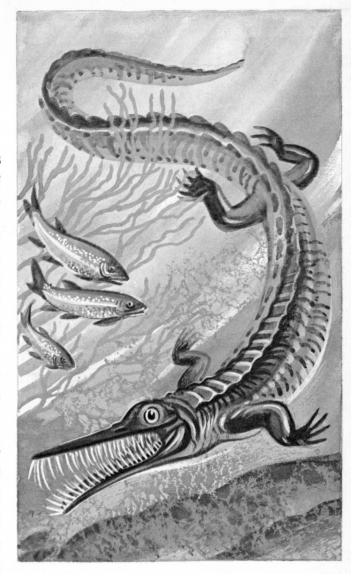

One usually thinks of the dinosaurs as land animals. But during the span of 120 million years in which dinosaurs of infinite variety spread out over the land, there were other reptiles that ruled in the sea and in the air. They were not dinosaurs, though they were distantly related, and some became nearly as large and fierce as the big dinosaurs.

Reptiles were the first creatures capable of living completely on land. Far back at the beginning of reptile history, some reptiles, after living on land and breathing air, moved from the land to the sea. They were still reptiles, but after millions of years their shape and look changed. They had to become more suited for a life in water. But the reptiles who went back to the water returned as reptiles, not as fish; they had no gills and they had no fins. Once having learned to breathe air, they continued to be air-breathers, replete with nostrils and lungs. The legs of the reptiles became paddles, or flippers—but not fins, even though they may have looked like fins. When the skeleton of a water reptile is studied, a limblike arrangement of bones in these paddles or flippers is revealed.

About 200 million years ago, during the Permian Period, fishlike reptiles began sharing the sea with fish. Sea reptiles such as the ferocious Sea Lizard (shown in the illustration) had already made a return trip from land to sea. They were about thirty inches long and bore a superficial resemblance to today's crocodiles. Despite the likeness, however, they are not their ancestors.

WERE WATER REPTILES MEAT-
OR PLANT-EATERS?

As they grew in size, sea reptiles began to look like immense fish, for the most part, but they remained reptiles and fed on fish. Some took on snakelike or eel-like forms, and resembled dragons or serpents of the sea. In shallow water, away from deep seas, early types of turtles swam about. Some of these turtles were also quite large. It is noted that one of them was over twelve feet in length and three tons in weight.

WHY DO SCIENTISTS
STUDY CROCODILES?

Today's crocodiles are a good deal like the ones who lived in the swamps 200 million years ago, except that the present-day specimens are smaller. The ancient great crocodiles were, in a manner of speaking, first cousins of the dinosaurs, and while some of them ventured forth into open sea in search of food, most of them seemed to stay close to shore, in the broad entrances of rivers, where they could attack slow-moving, dim-witted, plant-eating dinosaurs. Today's descendants of the great crocodiles, besides looking like prehistoric beasts, presumably must move about and act very much like them. Scientists are quite interested in the behavior of crocodiles and study them for clues that would reveal and perhaps even explain the actions of dinosaurs in those ancient eras.

WHERE AND WHEN WERE THE FIRST
SEA-REPTILE FOSSILS FOUND?

In the year 1811, twelve-year-old Mary Anning found a "dragon" on the English seacoast near the tiny village of Lyme Regis. It was actually a skeleton of fossil bones, approximately seven feet long. The creature had the skull and chest of a lizard, the snout of a dolphin, the teeth of a crocodile, the paddles of a whale, and the vertebrae (or backbone) of a fish. When found, it lay embedded in the blue slate composition of a cliff, and some men from the village had to be called to help Mary pry out the heavy stone. It was soon apparent that this was no ordinary find. The lord of the manor, to whom Mary took her find, paid her more than a hundred dollars for it and then submitted the fossil "dragon" to a museum for scientific study. Since it appeared to be a giant half-fish and half-lizard, scientists gave it the name *Ichthyosaur* (ɪᴋ-thee-uh-sor), which combined the Greek words for "fish" and "lizard."

Because the skeleton of the "fish-lizard" was the first creature of its type to be found, scientists spent a great deal of time studying it. Seven years passed before they even got around to naming it!

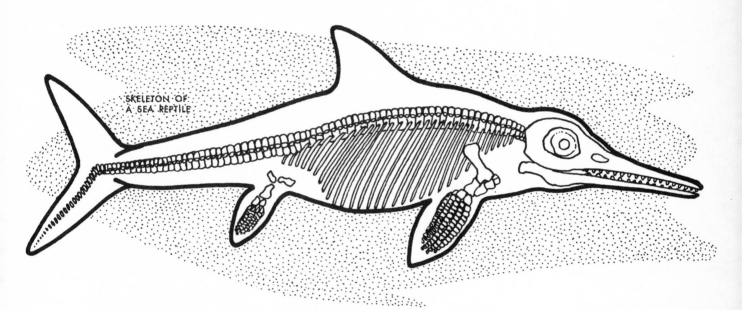

SKELETON OF
A SEA REPTILE

HOW DID SCIENTISTS FIND OUT WHAT ICHTHYOSAURUS REALLY LOOKED LIKE?

Ichthyosaurus was reconstructed by observation and deduction. By stretching an artificial "skin" over its bones, scientists saw that it had a shape like a lizard, with two large paddles in front and two very small ones in back. There was a long snout containing hundreds of teeth, and very large eyes. At its other end a long thin tail seemed to be broken and bent.

A scientist found another ichthyosaur's skeleton imbedded in a piece of slate. Working with engraving tools, small steel needles and picks, and even dental drills, the scientists began peeling and chipping off the slate in order to expose old bones. A project of this type often requires months of painstaking effort and patience.

In uncovering this skeleton, a scientist accidentally spilled a glass of water on the slate. When the water dried, it somehow left a dark outline around the skeleton, giving it the appearance of a colossal fish! It was all there—the submarine-shaped body, a long snout with teeth, no neck, a big tail fin—and, as an added surprise, a sail-shaped fin on top of his back.

HOW WERE ICHTHYOSAURUS BABIES BORN?

In later years, examination of ichthyosaur skeletons revealed another interesting characteristic: ichthyosaur eggs remained inside the female's body, hatched, and then young baby ichthyosaurs were born alive. The scientific term for this unusual process is to say that the ichthyosaur was ovoviviparous. This "jaw-breaker" word is derived from three Latin words —*ovum,* meaning "egg"; *vivus,* meaning "alive"; *parere,* meaning "to bring forth." (An egg-laying creature is termed oviparous; and one that gives birth to live young is termed viviparous.) The story of this remarkable creature, written in the rocks, was virtually complete.

WHO FOUND THE FIRST "NEAR-LIZARD"?

Mary Anning, whose discovery of the *Ichthyosaurus* skeleton assured her fame, continued collecting fossils and was subsequently rewarded with yet another find, the unearthing of the first plesiosaur (PLEES-ee-uh-sor), which means "near-lizard." The plesiosaur was described accurately—but not very scientifically—as "a snake strung through the body of a turtle." The name "near-lizard" is also not very accurate, but it was given to him because scientists theorized at first that he was a water creature developing into a lizard-like reptile. In reality, he was another land reptile who was moving into the sea.

Plesiosaurus had a body that was broad and flat, and paddled along near the surface of the water by means of long, finny feet that were something like oars. With his long snakelike neck and sharp-toothed jaws, he

Plesiosaurs pictured chasing after their food.

could strike out swiftly and snap up fish swimming many feet away. And once a fish was caught, there was no chance of escape!

This water-dwelling reptile sometimes reached a length of fifty feet. He has sometimes been described as a combination fisherman and rowboat.

ARE THERE SEA SERPENTS TODAY?

While the dinosaurs were clumping around on the land, there were some frightful reptile cousins in the sea that looked just like sea serpents. These creatures were sometimes 50 feet long. They had long necks and tails, and four large paddles. Their heads were small, but they had large jaws full of spiked teeth. As one of these monsters paddled around on the surface of the water, he would keep a sharp lookout for fish. When he saw one, the long snakelike neck would whip out, and quick as a flash the fish would be snapped up in strong jaws. No matter how slippery or wiggly the fish was, it couldn't escape, because the monster's teeth held it fast. *Elasmosaurus* (ee-lass-moh-SOR-us) was one of the largest of this kind to swim the seas. His name means "plated lizard."

The "sea-monster" reptiles all died out at about the same time—over 70 million years ago—but every once in a while people today claim that they have seen a "sea serpent." The reports are usually the result of an overactive imagination, or of an illusion of nature, or both. The only real ones that have turned up so far are the fossilized remains of creatures such as *Plesiosaurus*.

WERE FLYING REPTILES BIRDS?

Besides land and sea being filled with horrible monsters, even the air had dragon-like reptiles flapping through it. These were not true birds, even though they had wings and took to the air.

At first the flying reptiles were small—only about the size of a sparrow. But they were mean-looking little creatures with long jaws full of teeth. They had claws on their wings, and a long bony tail with a fin at the end of it.

DID FLYING REPTILES HAVE FEATHERS?

The later flying reptiles lost their teeth and most of their tail. But they had long pointed beaks, and a big crest of bone at the back of the head. Their wings, which had claws, were like glider wings of skin—these reptiles had no feathers.

The largest of these "flying dragons" was the size of a small airplane. His wingspread was 27 feet! Furthermore, all of these reptiles of the air were meat-eaters. They hunted small animals or fish from the air. Then they swooped down and snapped them up in their long jaws.

The world was a dangerous place in those days. There were "giants" on the earth, "monsters" in the sea, and "dragons" in the air!

WHAT WERE BAT-WINGED FLYING REPTILES?

Two typical flying reptiles whose wings might best be compared to those of present-day bats were *Rhamphorynchus* and *Pteranodon*.

Rhamphorhynchus (ram-fore-INK-us), which means literally "prow beak," lived in Central Europe about 130 million years ago. It was a flying lizard with an average wingspread of about four feet. (See illustration on page 48.)

Pteranodon (ter-AN-uh-don) means "toothless-wing." He had lost all his teeth—as is evident from his name—but as a substitute he had long beaklike jaws. At the back of his head, almost as a natural balance to his long pointed beak, was a long bony crest, or comb.

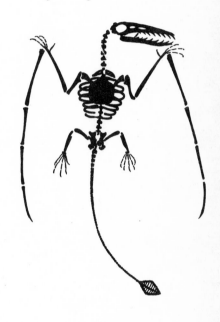

Pteranodon, who was one of the last of the flying reptiles, spent much of his time in the air. He was the size of a small airplane, having a wingspread of about twenty-seven feet, though it might be more accurate to say that he was a glider, for gliding is just what he did. With wings outstretched, *Pteranodon* must have looked like a giant kite in the sky, drifting with the winds and soaring with the rising warm-air currents. Oddly enough, his wings were really lengthy extensions of long fingers that had a weblike covering.

Below, skeleton of Rhampho-rynchus, a flying reptile; above, a view of the "arms," showing the extension of the fourth "finger."

Just as hawks do, *Pteranodon* sighted prey from a vantage point overhead and swooped down quickly to catch it. In his case, he caught fish and mollusks in his claws or by means of his long pointed snout. It is known that he had large eyes and very likely had the benefit of sharp vision for hunting his food. He also had a larger brain than most reptiles, a development brought about by his airborne movements and activity, which required greater balance and coordination than that needed by creatures depending on other forms of locomotion.

WHERE IN THE UNITED STATES WERE FOSSILS OF FLYING REPTILES FOUND?

Many specimens of *Pteranodon* have been found in Kansas, where the fossil remains were believed by Indians who first came upon them to be those of a supernatural creature. Sixty million years or more have passed since *Pteranodon* soared over the Upper Cretaceous sea of Kansas. He, himself, existed for almost that long—a period of fifty million years.

Ornitholestes (or-nith-o-LESS-tease), the "Bird-Stealer," about six feet long, was a flesh-eating reptile whose tail covered most of its length. It lived about 125 million years ago. Fossil remains were found in Wyoming in the United States. (See illustration on page 48.)

RHAMPHORHYNCHUS

PTERANODON

ORNITHOLESTES

WHAT WAS THE FORERUNNER OF BIRDS?

A fossil skeleton no larger than that of a crow was found in a limestone quarry in Germany in the year 1861. The bones were those of a reptile—yet etched in the smooth stone was a delicate impression of feathers. Scientists gave it the name *Archaeopteryx* (ar-kee-OP-ter-iks), from a combination of Greek words that translate as "ancient feather." Today there are birds in every part of the world, all believed to be the descendant of *Archaeopteryx*.

Archaeopteryx had a reptilian head, containing tiny teeth. His long tail was similar to that of a reptile, but it was edged with feathers. The wings had claws, but also feathers, which made an excellent wing surface and were infinitely more practical than the leathery skin of the "bat-winged" flying reptiles.

ARCHAEOPTERYX

WHAT WAS THE ADVANTAGE OF FEATHERS?

The long stiff feathers were a much-desired reinforcement. When the leathery skin of the bat-winged flying reptiles was torn or injured, it became totally useless; but when the feathers became damaged and dropped off, new ones would soon grow back.

Another significant feature of *Archaeopteryx'* feathers was that they insulated him. No matter how cold the weather, "Ancient Feather's" body heat did not escape to any great extent. It was a great accommodation, for by this time *Archaeopteryx* had become warm-blooded. In comparison, the scales of *Pterodactyls* could not by themselves retain body heat.

WHY DID THE DINOSAURS AND THEIR RELATIVES DISAPPEAR?

About sixty-five million years ago, after having ruled animal life for about 120 million years, dinosaurs became extinct.

When dinosaurs lived on earth, the climate was warm and mild everywhere. Then, very slowly, things began to change—the warm swamps dried up, the air became cooler, and new and different kinds of plants began to grow.

There were many animals that could adjust to these changes, and so they didn't die out. But the dinosaurs could not live in the new kind of world. They were cold-blooded, and they could not live comfortably in cool weather.

The plant-eaters could not eat the new kinds of plants, which had tougher stems and leaves. If the plant-eaters died out because their food had become scarce, it would affect the meat-eaters. They would die out, too, because they had to live on the plant-eaters.

DID ALL REPTILES DIE OUT?

The temperatures of the seas grew colder, just as the temperature of the air, and that might have killed off the water reptiles. But scientists are not completely satisfied with this explanation, because some reptiles managed to live on. Turtles, crocodiles, snakes and lizards are still with us to this day. Why was it just the dinosaurs and other reptile giants that couldn't live on?

Another explanation is the story of what happened to the dinosaurs' eggs. The big beasts laid their giant eggs right on the ground. They didn't hide them, or stay nearby to guard them. When the eggs hatched, the baby dinosaurs had to look after themselves. Other animals, including some of the smaller meat-eating dinosaurs, would get at the unprotected eggs. They made a fine, safe meal for a hungry little animal that had to hide from the big dinosaurs most of the time.

Many dinosaur eggs were surely destroyed in this way. But that alone could not have caused the whole dinosaur family to die out. The big sea reptiles died out at the same time, and their young were born alive in the water. So egg robbers cannot have been to blame completely.

Another idea is that there was a special kind of dinosaur sickness that killed the giants. Scientists wonder if there might not have been a disease that spread all over the world, affecting only dinosaurs and the big air and water reptiles. But then, why did it skip other reptiles?

Maybe the answer is a combination of all of these ideas. And maybe the warm-blooded furry mammals had something to do with it. They were a new kind of animal that had developed while the great dinosaurs ruled, but they were small and not important at first.

WHAT WERE THE ANCESTORS OF MAMMALS?

Several million years before the appearance of the first mammals, there was a medium-sized reptile, *Cynognathus* (sy-no-NAITH-us), which means "dog-jaw," that had some mammalian features. For this reason, *Cynognathus* is believed to be a direct ancestor of mammals. *Cynognathus,*

Several million years before the appearance of the first mammals, mammal-like reptiles such as Dicinodont, a herb-eater, and Cynognathus, a flesh-eater, roamed southern Africa.

about seven feet long, had teeth somewhat like those that mammals were to have; the canine teeth were lengthened and the tips of all the other teeth were sharper than the tips of reptiles' teeth. *Cynognathus* had strong legs and carried its body higher off the ground than reptiles do. What is more, its feet, like the feet of mammals, were beneath its body, instead of being extended out from the sides, as the legs of reptiles are. Unfortunately, we have not yet found the fossil skeletons of the animals that must link *Cynognathus* to the first true mammals.

DID MAMMALS LIVE DURING THE AGE OF DINOSAURS?

Toward the end of the reign of the reptiles, about 60 million years ago, the first mammals were scurrying over the land. But where the dinosaurs had huge bodies and tiny brains, the mammals had smaller bodies and larger brains. Few were larger than a terrier. The mammals were smarter and more active than the dinosaurs. And they were able to change more easily when the world changed.

HEAD OF PTILODUS

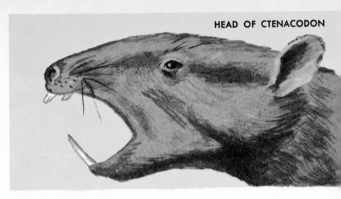

HEAD OF CTENACODON

WHAT IS A PREHISTORIC MAMMAL?

A mammal is a warm-blooded, four-limbed animal that is hairy or furry. Mammals are born alive, and newborn mammals are nursed on their mother's milk. Dogs, lions, horses, rabbits, seals, elephants, mice, and human beings are examples of mammals.

So, then, prehistoric mammals were warm-blooded, four-limbed, hairy or furry animals, born alive and nursed on their mother's milk in the ages before history was written.

When the great dinosaurs died out, the little mammals had the world for themselves. They have grown and developed, and mammals have been ruling the world ever since.

We live in the Age of Mammals which started about 70 million years ago. Although that is a very long time, it is not nearly as long as the Age of Dinosaurs.

WHAT WERE SOME MAMMALS THAT LIVED DURING THE AGE OF REPTILES?

Tiny jawbones which have been found provide the only clues to the physical appearance of the early mammals. From studying these, scientists have reconstructed models with the "most likely" look of these animals.

One of the mammals that lived during the Age of Reptiles was the *Ptilodus* (TILL-o-dus), which was about the size of a woodchuck. Two other, perhaps smaller, mammals were *Zalambdalestes* (za-lam-da-LESS-teez) and *Ctenacodon* (teen-ACK-o-don). Ptilodus was a plant-eater; the other two were insect-eaters. Little mammals such as these, in order to survive, had to keep out of the way of the ruling reptiles. Today, many little mammals are able to live in the Asian jungles by running and hiding from tigers, leopards, and other large meat-eaters. This is probably the way in which early mammals were able to live in the prehistoric jungles at the same time as the dominant reptiles.

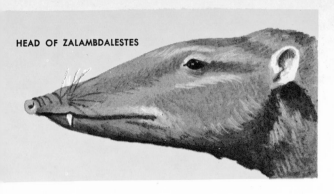

HEAD OF ZALAMBDALESTES

The only clues to the size and shape of early mammals are tiny jawbones which have been found and identified by scientists. The illustration shows (considerably enlarged) one of these fossil jawbones.

WHAT ARE "LIVING FOSSILS"?

Since mammals seem to have developed from reptiles, it is probable that, like reptiles, the first mammals hatched their young from eggs, as the modern duck-billed platypus does. We do not have direct evidence to prove this, but we do know that among the earth's first mammals were marsupials (mar-soo-pee-ils), animals that are born alive, but not fully developed. Newborn marsupials live the first part of their lives protected and nursed in a pouch attached to the mother animal. Kangaroos and opossums are present-day marsupials.

Marsupials appeared more than 100 million years ago, and during almost all of this great length of time, one kind of marsupial, the opossum, has been living. For this reason, opossums and platypuses are called "living fossils."

OPOSSUM

PLATYPUS

SOLENODON

WHAT ARE PLACENTAL MAMMALS?

Modern mammals are not only those that are living today, such as the ones that we see in zoos and circuses. Modern mammals also include those who lived as long as 60 million years ago.

The main way in which modern mammals are different from those like the duck-billed platypus or marsupials is that modern mammals give birth to live, fully-developed young. This kind of mammal is called a *placental* (pla-SEN-tl) mammal. Dogs, cats, horses, cows, rabbits, human beings, and nine-tenths of all other mammals living today are placental mammals.

Placental mammals appeared during the Age of Dinosaurs, not very long after marsupial mammals appeared. These early placental mammals, like the marsupials, have left a "living fossil" from which we can get an idea of what the first placental mammals were like. This "living fossil" is the solenodon that lives in Cuba and the Island of Hispaniola (Haiti and the Dominican Republic). A solenodon is about the size of a small cat.

Man now hunts the solenodon for its flesh, and the extinction of this animal is near. But how it managed to survive for more than 60 million years is a mystery.

NOTHARCTUS

WHAT WAS THE ANCESTOR OF THE LEMUR AND MONKEY FAMILY?

About 50 million years ago, in what is now Wyoming, a little mammal, the *Notharctus* (no-THARK-tus), ran and climbed about the forests in search of insects and fruits. The name of this little animal means "false bear," because its fossil was first thought to be that of a very small bear. *Notharctus* was about three feet long, half of which was the length of its tail. This tail probably could be curled about a tree branch in the same manner as a monkey's. *Notharctus* had a thin, foxlike face, large eyes, and finger-like grasping toes on all its four feet. It resembled a modern lemur, and, in fact, it is the oldest known ancestor of the family to which lemurs and monkeys belong. Compared with other animals of its time, *Notharctus* probably was very intelligent, because it had a large brain for its size.

Syndyoceras, a deerlike hoofed animal, lived about forty million years ago.

SYNDYOCERAS

PATRIOFELIS

MIACIS

WHAT WERE THE ANCESTORS OF THE CAT FAMILY?

Patriofelis (pat-ree-o-FEEL-is), or "father cat," which hunted in the forests and fields about 50 million years ago, was as big as a modern lion. Its skull was large, but its brain was not. It had massive jaws that held teeth adapted to slashing and shearing flesh. Its body was covered with coarse thick hair. Its legs were short and its toes widespread. It was not a fast runner, but it may have been a good swimmer because of its wide feet and long, thick tail.

Although *Patriofelis* is called the father cat, it has no living descendants. The real ancestor of all modern cats—lions, tigers, leopards, cougars, and others—is a small weasel-like animal, which was also the ancestor of all modern flesh-eating animals, *Miacis* (MY-ack-is). Its name means "small pointed," and refers to its teeth, the first flesh-cutting teeth among mammals. *Miacis* was about the size of a large squirrel. It had a large head, large ears, and a long tail. On each foot it had five toes, each bearing a sharp claw. The claws aided *Miacis* to climb trees and to catch and hold the animals on which it preyed.

WHAT WERE THE "THUNDER HORSES" OF THE INDIANS?

Sioux Indians, hunting bison in South Dakota and Nebraska, now and then found huge bones that had washed out of the earth during heavy rainstorms. Having no idea of extinct animals, the Sioux explained the great

55

BRONTOTHERIUM

bones by believing that they belonged to "thunder horses" that jumped from the sky to the earth during thunderstorms. Once on earth, the thunder horse used its powerful hoofs to kill bison. The huge bones really belonged to *Brontotherium* (bron-tuh-THEER-ee-um). This name means "thunder beast," and was given by a scientist who knew the Sioux legend.

The *Brontotherium* was fifteen feet long and stood eight feet high at the shoulder. At the end of its nose, it had a large flat horn made of bone. Although its kind existed for millions of years, they finally died out because they could not develop the type of teeth that were needed for eating the new and tougher grass that grew where *Brontotherium* lived.

WHAT ANIMALS ARE CONSIDERED TO BE THE ANCESTORS OF RACCOONS, WEASELS, BEARS AND DOGS?

About 35 million years ago, a small foxlike animal, *Cynodictis* (sigh-no-DICK-tis), lived in what today is South Dakota. The name means "dog stabber" and refers to the animal's sharp teeth. It is a descendant of *Miacis,* and together with one of his descendants, the *Daphoenodon,* became the ancestor of all dogs, bears, raccoons and weasels.

DAPHOENODON

CYNODICTIS

Daphoenodon (daf-EEN-o-don), whose name means "bloody tooth," hunted about five million years after *Cynodictis* in the western part of North America. It was about four-and-a-half feet in length. Its long, low-slung body, long tail, and short powerful legs were catlike, but it had a long wolflike head.

WHAT ANIMAL WAS THE LARGEST OF THE STABBING CATS?

About ten million years ago, the *Pliocene* (PLY-oh-seen) *Epoch* began, and with it came a gradual cooling, as the folding of the earth's crust raised the continents high and glaciers began to move down from the north. Pliocene means "more of the recent." It was during the Pliocene that the stabbing cats grew to be largest and fiercest. The largest of these was *Smilodon* (SMY-low-don), or "carving-knife tooth." The illustration on page 9 of this book shows a *Smilodon* attacking a *Mastodon* (MAS-tuh-don), a prehistoric elephant-like mammal that dwelled in the forests of eastern North America.

Smilodon is usually called a saber-toothed tiger, but tigers are biting cats that belong to the other branch of the prehistoric cat family. *Smilo-*

don was shorter than a modern lion, but it was more heavily built. Protruding from *Smilodon's* upper jaw were thick, pointed, nine-inch canine teeth. This stabbing cat had extremely powerful legs and muscular shoulders that enabled it to cling to its prey while the great saber-teeth slashed and stabbed. *Smilodon's* nostrils were located a little back from the end of its muzzle, so that this cat could breathe with its nose buried in the thick fur of its victims. How *Smilodon* chewed its food without its great stabbing teeth being in the way is an unsolved mystery.

WHY WERE SOUTH AMERICAN MAMMALS DIFFERENT FROM NORTH AMERICAN ONES?

Because South America was cut off from North America by the sea until the late Pliocene Epoch (the Pliocene Epoch lasted from eleven million to one million years ago), many strange mammals developed on the southern continent. For instance, there was the *Borhyaena* (bore-hy-EEN-a), a marsupial carnivore that looked much like a giant wolverine. Another marsupial carnivore was *Thylacosmilus* (thy-lack-os-MY-lus), a stabbing cat whose great fangs were protected by a flange of bone that jutted downward from the lower jaw. Also, there was *Toxodont* (TOX-o-dont), a heavy, clumsy, ten-foot-long plant-eater. The *Macrauchenia* (mack-raw-KEEN-ya) had a camel-like body, a long neck, and a short elephant-like trunk. One of the strangest of all the mammals to originate in South America was the *Glyptodont* (GLIP-toe-dont), an armored mammal. The largest of these mammals were fourteen feet long and five-and-one-half feet high. On the end of its tail was a spiked, clublike growth that may have been used as a weapon.

By the end of the Pliocene Epoch, North American mammals were

THYLACOSMILUS

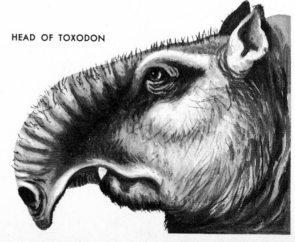

HEAD OF TOXODON

BORHYAENA

GLYPTODONT

MACRAUCHENIA

drifting through Central America to South America. Among these animals were carnivores like *Smilodon*. These flesh-eaters eventually wiped out most of the mammals they found in South America.

WHEN DID THE LAST OF THE PREHISTORIC MAMMALS DIE OUT?

Only a million years ago, the last Cenozoic epoch, the *Pleistocene* (PLICE-toe-seen), began. Pleistocene means "most of the recent." During this epoch the glaciers of the Northern Hemisphere reached their greatest southward advance. In all regions (except the tropical), the climate was cold. Four times the ice advanced, and four times it retreated. The last retreat began only 12,000 years ago, and is still going on. During the Pleistocene, the last of the truly prehistoric types of mammals died out. For instance, at the beginning of the Pleistocene, there lived in both North and South America a giant ground sloth called *Megatherium* (meg-a-THEER-ee-um), or "great beast." It was as large as an elephant, and could rear up eighteen feet from the ground to browse on the leaves of trees. About 10,000 years ago, the last of these giants died. *Smilodon* and *Megatherium* both died out, the last of the *Smilodons* living until 8,000 years ago.

GEOLOGICAL TIMETABLE AND INDEX

CENOZOIC ERA 60 MILLION YEARS	**CENOZOIC PERIOD** PLEISTOCENE EPOCH / PLIOCENE EPOCH / MIOCENE EPOCH / OLIGOCENE EPOCH / EOCENE EPOCH / PALEOCENE EPOCH — 1-60 MILLION YEARS AGO	MAN / AGE OF MAMMALS
MESOZOIC ERA 120 MILLION YEARS	CRETACEOUS PERIOD — 130 MILLION YEARS AGO / JURASSIC PERIOD — 155 MILLION YEARS AGO / TRIASSIC PERIOD — 185 MILLION YEARS AGO	AGE OF REPTILES
PALEOZOIC ERA 335 MILLION YEARS	PERMIAN PERIOD — 210 MILLION YEARS AGO / CARBONIFEROUS PERIOD — 265 MILLION YEARS AGO / DEVONIAN PERIOD — 320 MILLION YEARS AGO / SILURIAN PERIOD — 360 MILLION YEARS AGO / ORDOVICIAN PERIOD — 440 MILLION YEARS AGO / CAMBRIAN PERIOD — 520 MILLION YEARS AGO	AGE OF REPTILES / COAL AGE / AGE OF FISH / AGE OF INVERTEBRATES
PRE-CAMBRIAN ERA	600 MILLION YEARS AGO / 4-5 BILLION YEARS AGO / 4½ BILLION YEARS AGO / 5 BILLION YEARS AGO	AGE OF HIDDEN LIFE / NO LIVING THINGS / DEEP PART OF EARTH'S CRUST FORMED / APPROXIMATE BEGINNING OF EARTH AS PLANET